GW01406638

Original title:
The Magic of Christmas Love

Author: Julian Prescott
ISBN HARDBACK: 978-9916-90-982-9
ISBN PAPERBACK: 978-9916-90-983-6

Winter's Tender Touch

The snowflakes fall like feathers soft,
They stick to noses, then take off.
The sledding hill, a bumpy ride,
With tangled hats and snowball pride.

Hot cocoa spills, a chocolate mess,
With marshmallows vying for success.
The fireplace crackles, stories flow,
As Tippy the cat steals the show.

Radiance of the Season

The lights are twinkling on the tree,
As Santa's sleigh gets stuck, oh me!
The reindeer laugh, they start to dance,
While kids just giggle at the chance.

The cookies baked in shapes so weird,
With sprinkles, icing, and plenty of cheer.
A gingerbread house that looks like fun,
But ants declare it's theirs to run!

Festive Fables

A snowman stood with buttons wide,
But fell apart when kids did slide.
His scarf was red, his hat askew,
A sight that made the neighborhood coo.

The elves all laughed, they made a mess,
With glitter storms that left no less.
They wrapped the gifts, but with such glee,
Forgot that socks were 'just for me!'

Cherished Moments by the Fire

By the fire, we roast some treats,
Gooey marshmallows stick to our seats.
Dad tells a tale of how he slipped,
In winter boots that were surely equipped.

The dog snores loud, dreaming of bones,
While mom serves cookies, all warm and scones.
We cozy up in blankets too tight,
As dreams of snowmen fill the night.

New Beginnings in Flurries of White

Snowflakes dance like crazy on the ground,
Sleds are zooming, laughter's all around.
Bundles of joy in hats and mittens,
Hot cocoa's brewing, winter's never smitten.

Giant snowmen with carrots for noses,
Tickling the kids, as winter dozes.
Snowball fights lead to a frosty glint,
But mom's hot soup is the true winter hint.

Frosty windows to draw silly shapes,
We're creating a world with snow monster capes.
Chasing the dog through the cold snowy maze,
And giggling at snow angels' clumsy displays.

So raise your mugs, let the fun ignite,
New beginnings start with flurries of white!

Everlasting Bonds Beneath the Winter Sky

Under the stars where the chilly winds blow,
Friends huddle close, share stories, and glow.
Snowball poems tossed like hugs in the night,
Beneath the bright moon, everything feels right.

With scarves tied tight, we build a snow fort,
A kingdom of laughter, the best winter sport.
Each frosty breath like a cloud in the air,
As we make promises, in snowflakes we share.

The crackling fire sings to us near,
Hot marshmallows whisper friendship so dear.
Spontaneous dances in the soft, snowy flakes,
Creating memories that no winter breaks.

So here's to the moments, as magic takes flight,
Everlasting bonds beneath the winter sky bright!

Strings of Warmth in the Chill

In the cold, my socks have vanished,
But who needs toes, they're quite unhandy!
Sipping cocoa, marshmallows swim,
My dog's a blanket, furry and dandy.

He wags his tail, I can't complain,
Chasing yarn like a fluffy pain.
We cuddle close, a duo so bright,
In this chilly air, we spark delight.

Radiance of Love's Winter Glow

Snowflakes fall like feathers from a duck,
We giggle as they melt, what bad luck!
With hot cocoa spills, we start a race,
But it's the marshmallows that win first place!

We're warming toes by the fireplace glow,
Sharing tales of penguins that dance on snow.
You laugh so hard, I can't help but smirk,
In this chilly weather, love can really work.

Cup of Cheer, Heartfelt Near

Grab your cup, it's time to share,
Gingerbread men with a flair of flair!
Let's sing off-key, no high notes today,
With starlit giggles, we'll chase blues away.

Hot drinks spill, but we don't care,
As we dance 'round in winter's cool air.
Laughter hums, we're tangled like yarn,
With cups of cheer, our hearts are warm.

Tresses Twined Like Frosted Branches

Your hair's all knotted, like frosted twigs,
We laugh about it, no need for digs.
With each little braid, a story we weave,
Of snowball fights and what we believe.

Frosted branches outside look so fine,
Like little curls, they twist and twine.
We sip hot chocolate and share a grin,
Winter's a party; let our fun begin!

Holiday Wishes in Every Heart

In a sleigh pulled by a cat,
With a gift of cheese and a hat,
We'll spread cheer, so sweet and bright,
Unless the cat takes off in flight.

Tinsel tangled in my hair,
Three elves hiding under a chair,
Each gift wrapped with a giggle and grin,
Let's hope we've not mixed up the gin!

Cookies baked — a festive mess,
With sprinkles stuck in every dress,
The gingerbread men seem to move,
But it's just my dance skills that improve!

Come gather 'round, let's start to cheer,
With laughter loud enough to hear,
Here's to joy, let the fun impart,
Wishing holiday wishes in every heart!

Together in the Winter Wonderland

Snowflakes dance on my nose,
As I trip over my toes,
A snowman grins, he looks quite slick,
Did he steal my carrot? That's the trick!

Hot cocoa spills on my shirt,
But I drink it, doesn't hurt,
Sledding down the hill so steep,
I swear there's still a snowball in my heap.

Snowball fights, the gloves are soaked,
A freezing joke, oh how we croaked,
Together here, let's laugh and play,
In this winter wonderland, hooray!

With rosy cheeks and bright red mitts,
We'll make memories, those perfect fits,
Together we'll share this festive spree,
In snowflakes white, just you and me!

Delicate Flakes of Affection

Delicate flakes, oh what a sight,
Twirling gently in the light,
I caught one on my tongue — oh dear,
It's just another sneeze, I fear!

Bundled up in socks so warm,
With mismatched gloves that add to charm,
We twirl and spin like leaves in fall,
Then slip and land — right on the mall!

Chasing snowflakes, we take our chance,
What started as walking led to dance,
With giggles ringing, our hearts in sync,
We'll have to thaw out, I think!

So here's a toast to winter's grace,
With delicate flakes in every place,
With smiles so wide, let this be our fashion,
In this snowy season, let's spread affection!

Evergreen Quests for Warmth

In search of warmth, we embark,
On quests with cookies and a spark,
Evergreens whispering 'Please, don't trip!'
We dress like snowmen, what a rip!

The fireplace roars, we play it cool,
But our marshmallows are learning to drool,
S'mores in hand, and laughter shared,
We pretend we're chefs — but who really dared?

With blankets piled high on our chairs,
We tell ghost stories that flub and flare,
In cozy nooks with smiles and cheer,
Our evergreen quests bring friends near!

So gather 'round, let the warmth ignite,
Our hearts alight with silly delight,
For in every quest, together we chase,
The joy of the season, our happy place!

Tinsel Ties

Tinsel tangled in my hair,
I dance like I don't care.
Elves are laughing, what a scene,
Is this Christmas or a dream?

Mistletoe hangs overhead,
I kiss the cat instead.
Gifts wrapped poorly, bows askew,
Santa's got a lot to do!

Cookies burnt, a big mistake,
I meant to bake, but ate the cake.
Reindeer games on the roof,
I swear it's not all aloof!

Lights are flickering—oh dear!
Could it be that wine is near?
Tinsel ties and holiday cheer,
Bring on the fun and festive beer!

Sledding into Serendipity

Grab the sled, it's winter's call,
We're racing down, we'll never fall.
But here comes a bump, oh what a sight,
We're flying through snow, pure delight!

Snowflakes swirl, a grand parade,
Caught in a drift, our plans are made.
Laughter erupts, we can't take heed,
Is that a tree? Oh yes, indeed!

Hot cocoa waits at the bottom hill,
But first, let's slide for one more thrill.
Sledding into blissful space,
No other fun can match this pace!

When winter's chill makes us gleeful,
Every tumble feels quite lethal.
But joy and snow—what a mix!
Serendipity with sledding tricks!

Yuletide Wishes

Wishing stars and snowy nights,
Fluffy socks and pillow fights.
A Christmas tree that's leaning low,
With ornaments from years ago.

Cookies on plates, feel so grand,
But look! The dog's a gingerbread fan.
Wrapping paper all over the floor,
Who needs clean? We want more!

Santa's sleigh is flying high,
But forgot to wave goodbye.
A list of wishes, all in rhyme,
Just hope he comes before bedtime!

Yuletide cheer is here to stay,
With silly hats that lead astray.
So raise a glass, toast to delight,
Happy holidays, and sleep tight tonight!

Sugarplum Serenade

Sugarplums dance in my head,
While I stare at the cheese instead.
Twinkling lights all start to hum,
What's that noise? Oh, just my tum!

Dreaming of feasts, oh what a tease,
Chocolate cakes and grizzly cheese.
Under the stars, we find our song,
Everyone sings, though some sing wrong!

Rudolph's nose is shining bright,
Leading the way to the fridge tonight.
But wait, what's this? A jolly sight,
A cat in reindeer horns—oh what a fright!

Sugarplum dreams have come alive,
With every giggle, we all thrive.
So join the dance, let's take a chance,
In this sweet, festive, winter trance!

Shadows of Love Beneath the Boughs

Under the tree, we took a chance,
You tripped on roots in a silly dance.
Whispers of secrets, we softly spoke,
While squirrels laughed, oh what a joke!

Our shadows mingled in the cool air,
You said, "Is that your hair or a bear?"
I swatted at bugs, tried to act cool,
But all I could do was just play the fool.

The branches swung low, like they knew,
Our giggles were louder than morning dew.
With every glance, a playful shove,
Who knew that squirrels could fall in love?

As twilight came, we wrapped up tight,
In a blanket made of starlit night.
With shadows dancing, we made our vow,
Next time, let's skip the boughs for now!

Sweet Secrets Shared by the Fireside

By the fireside, we shared a tale,
Of a cat who thought she could sail.
You laughed so hard, you spilled your drink,
It splashed on a log, made the flames wink.

With marshmallows roasting, gooey delight,
You whispered, "Is that your foot or a bite?"
I snuck a s'more, my fingers got sticky,
And when you teased, it just made me picky.

We told ghost stories, but mostly we chuckled,
About that time I fell and got buckled.
The fire lit up our faces with cheer,
While flames danced along, new memories near.

And as the embers glowed soft and small,
You said, "This night beats a fancy ball!"
With laughter echoing, we made our way,
To sweet secrets shared, come what may.

Sugarplum Whispers in the Night

In the stillness, we whispered low,
About sugarplums and dances slow.
You said, "If I were a fruit, I'd be peach!"
But I'd much prefer a slice of quiche!

The moonlight cast its glow so bright,
We giggled at shadows, a silly sight.
You claimed your snoring could wake the dead,
While I plotted how to steal your bread.

With blankets piled high like a fort,
I dressed as a pirate, but you just snort!
We sailed the seas of our crazy dreams,
While the night hummed softly with moonlit beams.

So here we are, just you and me,
With sugarplum whispers and wide-eyed glee.
We'll dance in dreams 'til the morning sun,
In this silly world, we're always young!

The Glow of Togetherness in Every Corner

In every corner where laughter rings,
We find the joy that togetherness brings.
You danced like a chicken, oh what a sight,
While I cheered you on, heart full of light.

Under the couch, a dust bunny roams,
With you and me, it feels like home.
We made our own rules, it's plain to see,
The weirder the better, just you and me!

The glow of the fridge lights our late-night snacket,
You searched for treats, but found an old racket.
We laughed 'til we cried, it's a nightly chore,
Togetherness shines when you open that door.

So here's to the moments, both silly and bright,
With you by my side, everything's right.
In every nook and cranny, I see the score,
Our love's the glow that keeps wanting more!

Love's Brightest Winter

In winter's chill, you stole my heart,
With snowflakes falling, a perfect start.
You wore a scarf, so bright, so warm,
But lost your hat—oh, what's the harm?

We built a snowman, round and stout,
But he fell down, we laughed, no doubt.
We skied together, you fell in a drift,
Now you claim you're a snowball gift!

You made me hot cocoa, so rich and sweet,
But you spilled it all—what a funny feat!
We snuggled close beneath starry skies,
With marshmallows floating, oh, what a prize.

So this winter love, that makes us grin,
Is brighter than lights, let the fun begin!

Whispered Wishes on Frosty Nights

Frosty nights, you whispered my name,
But sneezed right after, it's part of the game.
We snuggled closely, wrapped up tight,
Then spilled the popcorn—oh, what a sight!

You wished on a star, then had to ask,
What's for dessert? A daunting task.
With cookies baking, the kitchen's a mess,
But your flour face gives me great happiness!

Snowflakes twirl, as we sip hot tea,
You added a dash of too much glee!
Now we're giggling, it's hard to stop,
Your silly dance makes my heart go plop.

So here's to wishes on nights so cold,
With laughter and warmth, our story unfolds!

Hearts Wrapped in Silver Ribbon

Hearts wrapped up tight in a silver bow,
Stumbling through life, a bit too slow.
We play hide and seek in our cozy space,
But I lost my socks—you've got my face!

We toast with mugs of steaming delight,
But you spilled yours—it was quite the sight.
We gaze at the stars, but then you trip,
Fell in the bushes, oh what a slip!

With ribbons and bows, our love's all aglow,
We dance in the kitchen, put on quite the show.
With laughter and chaos, we hold each other tight,
Two silly hearts wrapped in love's pure light.

Joyful Spirits in the Night

The moon is bright, the stars are bold,
We danced around, our moves uncontrolled.
With socks that slip and laughter loud,
We twirled like leaves, so free and proud.

A cat jumps high, a dog runs fast,
In this wild party, none are outclassed.
We giggle at jokes that make no sense,
Like why the chicken crossed, it's all pretense!

Hot cocoa spills on worn-out clothes,
A crocodile in slippers strikes a pose.
The fire crackles, so does our cheer,
Together we'll sing till the morning's near.

So raise your mug to joyous nights,
Where spirits soar and laughter ignites.
We'll dance till dawn, with hearts so light,
In this funny, magical, starry night.

Hearthside Harmony

By the fireplace, we roast marshmallows,
Mom's burnt them all—what a bunch of fellows!
Dad tells tall tales of his youth so wild,
While little Timmy giggles, the silly child.

The cat claims the spot, a throne made of fur,
While the dog plots mischief with a soft purr.
The couch is a ship, sailing seas of cheer,
Each wave brings laughter, and friendly jeer.

Grandpa snores loud, his tales cut short,
While Grandma's knitting, a colorful sport.
With socks full of holes, and hearts full of glee,
Our hearthside gatherings are all we need to be.

So let's sing a tune, let's play charades,
In the warmth of love, the fun never fades.
With cookies and hugs, we'll stay up all night,
In this cozy chaos, everything feels right.

Mistletoe Murmurs

Under the mistletoe, we stand in line,
A kiss from Aunt Betty? Oh, how divine!
With peppermint breath and awkward dreams,
We laugh at the moment, bursting at seams.

Cousins are sneaky, trying to peek,
At all the shenanigans, funny and bleak.
We whisper old secrets but cackle with cheer,
At the sight of Uncle Joe in holiday gear.

A sprig of mistletoe—what a crazy sight,
A grandpa's surprise for this starry night.
With giggles and blushes, we give it a go,
And suddenly Aunt Sally steals the show!

So gather around, share laughter and cheer,
For mistletoe murmurs bring love ever near.
With jingle bells ringing and hearts feeling bright,
This festive confusion feels just so right.

Radiant Hearts in the Snow

Snowflakes swirl like a magical dance,
We trip and we tumble, not a second chance.
Snowmen with carrots, a silly chic hat,
We all shout with glee, while the dog chases that!

Sledding down hills, we're flying so high,
With giggles and shrieks that echo the sky.
But watch out! Here comes a surprise snowball,
It's Fred with his aim—he's not subtle at all!

Hot chocolate ready, marshmallows galore,
We huddle inside, our toes feeling sore.
With winter tales shared, we drink and we cheer,
Warmed by the laughter, our hearts drawing near.

So let's make some memories, so merry and bright,
With radiant hearts in this snowy delight.
In the joy of the season, we're never alone,
In the laughter and love, we've forged our own home.

A Touch of Love in Every Ornament

On the tree, the tinsel gleams,
With all my hopes and dreams.
I hung a sock, it's full of snacks,
Just in case the elves relax.

The star on top is slightly askew,
It hides my misshapen glue.
Each bauble tells a silly tale,
Like when my cat stole the mail.

Lights that twinkle, flicker, and dash,
I swear they're having a bash!
And when I dance around the floor,
Some ornaments seem to implore.

So here's to love, wrapped in a bow,
And snacks from Santa, just for show.
With laughter shared and hangers bent,
A touch of love, 'tis heaven-sent!

Giggles Beneath the Falling Snow

Snowflakes swirl like tiny clowns,
Blanketing the sleepy towns.
I trip and fall, it's no surprise,
With snow-filled boots and frosty thighs.

The snowman grins, it's made of snow,
His carrot nose steals the show.
He wears my scarf, can you believe?
I think he'll stay here till I leave!

Kids now throw snowballs with glee,
Meanwhile, I sip hot cocoa tea.
Laughter rings, as snowflakes descend,
In this winter scene, joy has no end.

Beneath the snow, the world's a stage,
We slip and slide, yet we engage.
For laughter is the best of cheer,
In every flake that draws us near!

The Firelight of Shared Glances

By the fire, we sit and toast,
Who knew marshmallows could boast?
A glance turned warm, then oh so shy,
As sparks drift up into the sky.

Your cheesy grin lights up the night,
The popcorn bowl, such a delightful sight.
Soon we're laughing till we snort,
Jokes fly high; it's quite the sport!

Crackling flames echo our fun,
In this glow, we've surely won.
Games of silly truth or dare,
With hearts aflame, we breathe the air.

So let's embrace these moments dear,
With warmth and whimsy, we have no fear.
For love and laughter dance so bright,
In firelight, our hearts take flight!

Snow-Dusted Dreams of You and Me

Whispers of dreams wrapped in white,
In a world that feels just right.
Snowflakes twirl, oh what a sight,
As we snuggle in cozy delight.

We build a fort, our secret place,
With snowball fights at a breakneck pace.
In the chaos, we laugh and yell,
Soon warm cocoa in our great shell.

You stick out your tongue for a flake,
I laugh as I try not to shake.
With a smile wider than winter's chill,
Our hearts dance freely, how they thrill!

Beneath the stars, our dreams take flight,
In snow-dusted magic, everything's right.
So here's to you, my snowy muse,
In winter's embrace, we never lose!

Shared Laughter in the Snow

Snowflakes falling, soft and light,
Kids bundled up, what a sight.
Snowballs flying, laughter loud,
Giggles echo, it's a crowd.

Sleds are racing down the hill,
Who will fall? Oh, what a thrill!
Face-first in snow, they tumble down,
Covered in white, without a frown.

Hot cocoa spills, a marshmallow fight,
The dog leaps up, what a delight!
Snowmen built with carrot noses,
Winter fun, in all its poses.

So let's all share this snowy cheer,
With frosty smiles, we hold dear.
Together we laugh in pure delight,
In this winter wonderland, so bright.

Love Letters Stamped with Snowflakes

I sent you a letter, in winter's embrace,
With snowflakes dancing, a loving trace.
Each line wrapped in frosty delight,
I hope it arrives on a snowy night.

Your fragrance lingers like fresh pine,
I scribbled 'I love you' in every line.
The postman slips on icy ground,
As love letters swirl all around.

I stamped it with kisses, in icy flair,
But it sailed away on a winter's air.
Does love float better through snow or rain?
These thoughts are crazy, but just the same.

A response from you, I long to see,
Perhaps you'll pen back, "You're my cup of tea."
In this snowy season, let's embark,
On love's wild journey, a light in the dark.

Embracing the Essence of Winter's Kiss

Winter's kiss is crisp and bright,
Whispers frosty, pure delight.
The breath we see like little ghosts,
Chasing warmth, that's what we'll toast.

Scarves wrapped tight, such style we flaunt,
Snow boots making us look like a font.
Hot soup bubbling on the stove,
In winter's arms, we love to rove.

Icicles hang like glassy tears,
While snowflakes dance amidst our cheers.
A chilly embrace, oh so sweet,
With you beside me, I feel complete.

So let's bundle up, bravely roam,
Through winter's magic, we find our home.
In every chill, there's warmth I see,
In winter's kiss, it's you and me.

Celebration of Love in Every Heartbeat

Your heartbeat's rhythm, oh so fine,
Like soft drumming on Valentine.
In every pulse, I hear the sound,
A love song, in joy we're bound.

Dancing close, we spin and sway,
In winter's chill, we find our play.
The wind carries laughter, sweet and bright,
As we celebrate love, our hearts take flight.

With every hug, we push back cold,
Wrapped together, brave and bold.
The frosty air can't freeze our spark,
We shine together, just like art.

So let's toast to love, in every beat,
With snowflakes falling beneath our feet.
In this grand celebration, I confess,
My love for you is pure, no less.

Starlit Serenades of Affection

Underneath the moon's bright glow,
I tripped and fell right on my toe.
The stars above just laughed so wide,
As I clutched my foot and cried with pride.

In love's embrace, we shared a dance,
But then you sneezed; oh, what a chance!
A sprightly twirl turned into flight,
I landed in a tree, what a sight!

Your laughter echoed through the night,
As squirrels looked down with sheer delight.
Romance is grand, but let's take care,
Next time, let's swing with more flair!

Now every star feels like a tease,
Reminding me of that rogue sneeze.
With every love song sung out there,
I'll never dance without a prayer!

Joyful Echoes of Yuletide Hearts

Snowflakes fall like fuzzy socks,
While I trip over all the blocks.
The tree is bright, the lights on cue,
But where's the eggnog? I need some too!

Carols ring from door to door,
But who knew I was tone-deaf for sure?
I sang so loud, the dog just fled,
Now he hides beneath the bed!

The cookies baked, well, burnt instead,
My icing skills? A dread, misled.
Yet laughter fills this home of cheer,
So we toast with cider, full of cheer!

In joyful echoes, hearts collide,
With friend and family by our side.
One last laugh before night's end,
Next year, I promise to attend!

Frost-Kissed Promises Softly Spoken

Winter's chill can freeze your toes,
Yet here I am, in shorts, who knows?
A snowman waves, his carrot nose,
I thought it was a pretty rose!

As frost-kissed whispers fill the air,
I asked you if you'd like to share.
But all I got was icy breath,
Guess romance can lead to chilly death!

Sledding down the hill, so grand,
I ate more snow than I had planned.
Your giggles echoed with the breeze,
I'm pretty sure I flew with ease!

By the fire, we warmed our hearts,
With marshmallow fluff and bad charts.
Here's to winter and to us,
Next time, I'll wear shoes—no fuss!

A Symphony of Warmth in the Cold

Outside it's frosty, icy, gray,
But I'm wrapped up like a rogue bouquet.
My scarf's too long, it trails behind,
I trip, I fall, it's so unkind!

Hot cocoa in my mismatched cups,
While your dance moves make me erupt.
You sprinkle cheer like snowflakes bright,
But how'd you end up in that light?

The world outside is cold as ice,
But in here? Well, it feels quite nice.
With laughter warm and hearts so bold,
We create a tale that's yet untold!

So here's to warmth, let's take a chance,
In this wacky winter dance.
With every giggle and twirl we make,
Our symphony never goes to break!

Soft Hues of Love Against White Backdrops

In a world of gray and white,
I found a heart that's oh so bright.
With soft hues dancing in the air,
We painted love without a care.

Your laughter splashes like paint,
A joyful scene, nothing quaint.
I tried to tell you, my dear mate,
That love's a canvas, not too late!

Together we splatter, what a sight!
Your heart's my easel, it feels just right.
With every brushstroke, we create
A masterpiece, oh, isn't fate great?

So here we are, in colors bold,
Telling stories that never get old.
In soft hues against the white,
Our love's a rainbow, pure delight!

Secret Santa's Heartfelt Tokens

Twas the night of gifts and glee,
Who wrapped this hideous tree?
A sweater knitted from two left hands,
My Secret Santa surely understands!

A candle that smells like socks gone bad,
Oh, what a thoughtful gift, I'm glad!
Is this a prank, or pure affection?
Next year, I'll aim for perfection!

The cookies too, they crumbled down,
All the joy turned to a frown.
But as I laughed and chewed on glue,
I realized my friends made it too!

So here's to gifts that make no sense,
Wrapped with love, just like a fence.
In laughter, joy, and silly fun,
Secret Santa, you've truly won!

Close Enough to Catch a Snowflake

Walking in the chilly air,
You caught a snowflake in your hair.
I reached to pluck it, oh so sweet,
And tripped right over my own feet!

We laughed and rolled in winter's snow,
A couple of clowns, don't you know?
With frosty noses and red cheeks,
Your smile's the warmth my heart seeks.

The snowflakes danced like little stars,
While I dodged snowballs from near and far.
You threw one my way, a target dandy,
I retaliated—oh, how wandy!

So while we catch the flurries bright,
We're creating memories in the night.
With every flake, our love does grow,
In winter's wonderland, let's steal the show!

Nighttime Carols and Loving Lyrics

In the dark, our carols soar,
But who knew I could hit that score?
Off-key notes fill up the air,
Your laughter twinkles everywhere!

We sing of love, the moon as our guide,
As cats join in for a joyful ride.
Crazy rhythms that only we know,
Like a duet turned solo show!

The stars above, they seem to wink,
At every note, we pause and think.
The lyrics slip but that's just fine,
Your hand in mine makes it divine!

So here's to nights of songs gone wrong,
With hearts that sing to their own song.
In every note, I find my bliss,
With you, my love, how could it miss?

Snow-globe Sentiments

In a snow globe, things may freeze,
But my love for you is sure to please.
Shake it up and watch it swirl,
Just like our life—what a crazy whirl!

I saw a snowman wearing a hat,
He looked at me and thought, 'What's that?'
I laughed so hard, I started to snort,
Should have seen him—he's made of port!

Snowflakes falling, landing on nose,
I'm no expert, but hey—who knows?
When winter comes, we play all day,
Hot chocolate sips keep cold at bay!

As snowdrops dance and pitter-pat,
I make a snow angel, flat as a mat.
With mittened hands and cheeks aglow,
Winter's a blast, let's enjoy the show!

Warmth Beneath the Stars

Under the stars, we dance out of tune,
Twinkling lights look like a cartoon.
With marshmallow dreams and cosmic chills,
We roast great stories that give us thrills!

Trying to star gaze with lots of dispute,
You think that's Venus? Nah, bro, it's fruit!
Let's sing to the moon, we know all the songs,
Hope it don't mind our off-key throngs!

Under the blanket, it's cozy and tight,
You say you're cold? Darling, hold me right!
With cheeks all aglow beneath the night sky,
We giggle at meteors, oh how they fly!

Found a shooting star, it wasn't a plane,
Wished for more snacks, can't share the gain.
With laughter and warmth in starry embrace,
Let's capture this moment, it's our happy place!

Holiday Hearts Unfold

Tangled in lights, what a sight to see,
Oh how the ornaments tumble, whee!
With cookies heaped high, we jam and munch,
But Mom's secret stash? That's our ninja lunch!

Wrapping up gifts, I can't tie a bow,
With tape on my fingers, I move too slow.
But when the paper flies—all shreds and tears,
The chaos brings laughter, oh who even cares?

Stockings hung with hope and cheer,
But why's my sock stuffed with a deer?
Presents galore, what a holiday race,
Can't wait for chocolates to vanish without trace!

As carols ring loud, we sing off-key,
But festive spirit sings harmony!
With hearts wide open, and joy on parade,
Here's to the laughter, let's never evade!

Glimmers of Togetherness

In a room full of chaos, we find the glow,
Like fireflies buzzing in a soft flow.
With laughter shared over silly old tales,
We cheer through life; love never pales.

Candles flicker, the shadows prance,
But we just laugh, not missing a chance.
To twirl and skip with silly delight,
Creating memories that ignite our night!

Fuzzy socks on and hot tea in hand,
We giggle at life, so perfectly planned.
With glitter and sparkles all around,
In this togetherness, true love is found!

Through ups and downs, we navigate rolls,
Like a rollercoaster with joyful trolls.
Here's to the glimmers, both near and far,
For together we shine, no matter how bizarre!

Hot Cocoa and Heartfelt Glances

Hot cocoa steaming in our hands,
Marshmallows floating like tiny plans.
You wink at me, I spill my drink,
Your laughter makes me start to think.

We sip and giggle, spill it all,
Chocolate mustache on your call.
You say, "It's just a fashion choice,"
I snort and nearly lose my voice.

So here we are, with mugs in tow,
A chocolate tide that steals the show.
With every glance, the world's awry,
We melt like cocoa, oh my my!

But who needs warmth from liquid gold,
When love's the drink that never gets old?
Your smile's the spark that warms me through,
In this sweet cup, it's me and you!

Festive Echoes of Embracing Souls

The bells are ringing, tunes in flight,
My dancing feet, oh what a sight!
You step on toes and laugh with glee,
Admit it, love, you dance like me!

The snowflakes twirl, a flurry bright,
You trip and fall, oh what a fright!
But then you grin, and wave your arms,
A snowman bod that brings such charms.

We share warm hugs, a twinkling spree,
Goofing around, we're wild and free.
"Let's build a fort!" I shout with cheer,
But we end up with a laughter sphere.

In festive echoes, hearts collide,
With every giggle, you're my guide.
From snowy nights to joyful days,
In our embrace, forever stays!

Boughs of Holly and Tender Touches

The holly boughs hang high on show,
While mistletoe whispers, "Come and go!"
You tiptoe near, I bat my eye,
But sneak a peck and watch you fly!

Decked out in tinsel, wrapped too tight,
You trip on lights, a comical sight.
I stifle chuckles, hold my breath,
We're tangled now, be careful, lest!

But in your grip, I find my place,
With every fumble, I adore the chase.
Boughs of holly? They're just for show,
Your chaotic charm steals the whole show.

So let's embrace this silly dance,
Forget the rules, just take a chance.
With tender touches, giggles unfold,
In this laughing tale, our hearts grow bold!

Chimes of Laughter in the Snow

The snowflakes fall, a gentle knell,
In frosty air, our joy will swell.
You throw a snowball, hit my hat,
I laugh and run—oh please, not that!

Our chimes of laughter fill the air,
With every slip, a winter dare.
You link your arm, a guide so strong,
Together, love, we can't go wrong.

We build a castle, flurry high,
But it collapses, oh my, oh my!
Your eyes are bright, like stars that glow,
In this silly chaos, hearts just flow.

So here we are, in snowy dreams,
Where every giggle bursts at the seams.
With chimes of laughter in the snow,
In winter wonder, love will grow.

Wreaths of Warmth

A wreath on the door, it's looking quite round,
With bits of old tinsel and leaves on the ground.
It beckons to squirrels, a feast in its sight,
They nibble and scamper, what a silly sight!

The wind sings a tune, a frosty old song,
While the wreath starts to wobble, it won't last long.
Each bow is a challenge, a knot you can't lose,
But somehow I'm tangled in ribbons and blues!

The neighbors peek over, they're curious too,
As I wrestle with garland, all shades of bright blue.
They chuckle and giggle, it brings them delight,
While I wrestle with wreaths, oh what a sight!

So hang up your wreaths, your silly decor,
Embrace all the chaos, who cares anymore?
With laughter and love, we'll make it all right,
For joy's in the chaos, it sparkles so bright!

Twinkling Hope

In the dark of the night, lights start to glow,
With twinkling intentions, they put on a show.
Each bulb is a dream, some wish and some pray,
They dance in the darkness, come join in the play!

So many colors, it looks like a zoo,
Red, green, and yellow, which one should I do?
Then flicker, then flash, oh could it be true?
More lights than I planned, where am I to strew?

The neighbors complain, they can't find their beds,
With winks from the bulbs, my excitement spreads.
It's a twinkling headache, this festive display,
But my heart is just singing, oh what a wild fray!

So let's deck out our homes, with dreams in the air,
Each twinkling light shares a laugh and a dare.
For hope that we shine, in the night so profound,
With lights all around, joy's meant to astound!

Candlelight Connections

A candlelit dinner, what could go wrong?
The wax drips a river, a sweet-smelling song.
I fumble my fork, and my drink takes a dive,
Oh what a clumsy way—do I need to revive?

The flickering flame casts shadows on walls,
My date's face is wrinkled, as laughter befalls.
The food is now cold, but we're warming our hearts,
With every misstep, a memory starts!

With flickering lights, we craft our own tale,
Of wax wars and giggles, a laugh that won't pale.
The meal's just a backdrop, our hearts take the lead,
In candlelight chaos, together we're freed!

So here's to connections, in laughter we find,
With candles and chaos, the mess is divine.
For love's not perfection, it's laughter in tow,
In candlelight moments, together we glow!

Snowflakes of Devotion

Snowflakes are falling, like bits of confetti,
I'm bundled up warmly, my scarf's oh so heavy.
Each flake is a promise, unique as can be,
But somehow they stick to my nose, can't you see?

I twirl and I tumble, a frosty ballet,
While snowflakes keep landing, they want me to stay.
With a slip and a slide, I'm lost in the freeze,
But oh, how I marvel, I'm filled with such ease!

The snowmen arise, with eyes made of rocks,
Each hat's a bold statement—a show of odd socks.
They stand there so proudly, my wintertime friends,
In snowflakes of laughter, the joy never ends!

So dance with the flurries, embrace every fall,
For snowflakes of love, they blanket us all.
Let's treasure these moments, in warmth and in cheer,
With snowflakes of devotion, there's nothing to fear!

Footprints in the Snow

In the snow, my footprints show,
A path that leads where? I don't know!
Squirrels point and laugh, oh what a sight,
My moonwalk skills give them quite a fright.

I tripped and fell, and oh, what a mess,
Fluffy snowflakes turned into a dress.
With every step, I slip and slide,
Looks like winter's won this joyride!

My footprints tell tales, some silly, some grand,
Like a clumsy dancer at a winter band.
I swear I saw a rabbit tap his toe,
Judging my style; oh, the ego will grow!

But the joy of winter is hard to ignore,
With each flake that falls, I just want more.
So I'll frolic and play, let the snowflakes fall,
Leaving footprints of laughter, the best mark of all!

Marks of Love

Hearts drawn in the fog, oh what a scene,
A smudged little "I love you" in-between.
With quirky doodles, we share our art,
Each scratchy line a page to my heart.

Coffee stains and crumbs, love turns a mess,
Chocolate kisses are all I confess.
We make silly faces, and silly puns,
In the gallery of us, we're top-notch fun!

In spilled your drink, oh what a joke!
Loving the chaos, this heart's not broke.
With laughter and hugs, our canvas gets bright,
These marks of love make everything right!

So let's paint the world with our silly quirk,
Our love is the work of a true artist's perk.
We'll scribble our tales, both messy and sweet,
In this life of ours, no love is complete!

A Tapestry of Joy on Winter Nights

In winter's weave, the joy begins,
With hot cocoa smiles and snowball wins.
A tapestry crafted with laughter and cheer,
Under the stars, the best time of year.

Knitted mittens, and a hat that's too tight,
Dancing in circles, what a pure delight!
With snowflakes falling, we twirl around,
In the joy of this night, happiness is found.

We'll bundle up bright, look silly, and play,
A ski trip disaster? Just another day!
Wrapped in each other, we share all the fun,
With winter's embrace, we shine like the sun.

So let's build a snowman, give him a name,
With a carrot for a nose, we'll sing out his fame.
A tapestry woven tight with delight,
In winter's sweet glow, our hearts take flight!

Hearts Chiming Like Silver Bells

With every jingle, our hearts entwine,
Like silver bells ringing, you're truly divine.
We dance through the night, with glee and with flair,
Your laughter's a melody, floating in the air.

We twirl and we spin, like leaves in the breeze,
Your love is my anthem, my heart's favorite tease.
In this lovely chorus, we both play a part,
The sweetest symphony, a song from the heart!

Oh, let's make it festive, with tinsel and cheer,
Each note that we share, brings you ever near.
With hearts chiming bright, we're a joyful duet,
Our love's a fine tune, I'll never forget.

As the bells keep ringing, we cherish this sound,
In this dance of laughter, our spirits are found.
With silver bells chiming, our hearts will declare,
Together forever, love's song fills the air!

Afterglow of Moments Under the Stars

Under the stars, we lay side by side,
With giggles and dreams, we laugh and confide.
In the afterglow, love's sparkles ignite,
A comedy show on a blanket at night.

Beneath cosmic wonders, our thoughts take flight,
With alien stories, we imagine the night.
Sipping moonlight, with each playful glance,
The universe spins, and we're lost in this dance.

Counting the stars, as we drift in delight,
Your laughter's the best guide in the dark of night.
We'll share all our hopes, our wishes collide,
In this afterglow world, let's take a ride!

So here's to the moments that glimmer and shine,
Under the stars, how lucky you're mine!
With every shared giggle, my heart's set to spark,
In this afterglow magic, together, let's embark!

Winter's Caress and Heartfelt Embrace

Winter's here, oh what a sight,
The snowflakes dance, all pure and white.
I lost my hat, it blew away,
Now I'm freezing, what can I say?

Hot cocoa spills, it stains my coat,
I thought I'd swim, but I can't float.
The sled's a blast, but wait, oh no!
I hit a tree, and down I go!

Frosty breath, it leaves a mark,
I tried to skate, but fell in the park.
With cheeks like apples, bright and red,
We laugh and dream of warm beds ahead.

So here's to winter, for all its cheer,
With slips and falls, let's hold it dear.
Through icy fun, and hot chocolate seams,
In winter's arms, we find our dreams.

Family Ties Tightly Woven

Gather 'round, it's family time,
Where chaos reigns, but love's in rhyme.
Uncle Joe's jokes are such a hit,
And Auntie Sue just spilled her grit.

Cousins wrestling on the floor,
Grandma's knitting, whispers galore.
The dog dashes in, steals a shoe,
While Mom preps dinner, asking 'who's who?'

Board games clash, the points are rigged,
Sisters roll dice, their faces big.
Laughter echoes through the halls,
While someone's making water calls!

Through all the mess, we cherish each hug,
Family ties are kind of snug.
With food and fun, the heartbeats race,
In this wild love, we find our place.

The Hush of Snow

Snowflakes fall without a sound,
Blanketing streets, a silent crown.
Neighborhood kids all bundle tight,
Deep in dreams of snowy delight.

I built a snowman, oh what a face,
With carrots and buttons, a snowy grace.
But then it melted, what a shame,
My frosty buddy, gone… no blame!

Fireplaces crackle, warmth inside,
As outside, snowflakes twist and glide.
Hot tea in hand, the blankets close,
In winter's hush, the comfort grows.

So here's to snow, it brings such peace,
With every flake, our laughter's lease.
In this gentle, frosty embrace,
We find our joy, our happy place.

The Warmth of Us

In chilly nights, together we glow,
Snuggled on couches, you and me know.
With popcorn popping and films to share,
We laugh so loud, without a care.

Funny faces, pillow fights,
Silly moments, pure delights.
With every joke and playful tease,
Home feels warm, like summer breeze.

Friends like blankets, cozy and tight,
We dance through the chaos, all feels right.
In our bubble, the world's okay,
With a twist and a turn, we laugh all day.

So here's to warmth, to love that binds,
Through every season, in heart and minds.
With memories made that keep us strong,
We cherish this life, where we belong.

Angelic Voices in Harmony

In the choir loft, we take our stance,
But when we sing, it's quite a dance.
Off-key notes fly, like ducks in a row,
Harmony's dream is a comical show.

Sister's too loud, brother's so low,
The cat joins in with a frantic meow.
With laughter ringing, we try once more,
The neighbors peek in, what's this uproar?

Every note brings a chuckle and cheer,
As we belt out tunes, distractions near.
In our off-key world, we find our bliss,
With voices of joy, how can we miss?

So let the music play loud and free,
In this happy chaos, just you and me.
With angelic voices, though a bit shy,
We sing from the heart, and it's worth the try.

Hearts Alight with Seasonal Splendor

Snowflakes dance like they're in a trance,
Every snowman wears not just a chance.
With scarves so bright and noses so round,
We laugh and cheer, joy can be found.

The trees are decked in colors bright,
Even the squirrels are dressed for the night.
Each cookie baked, a festive delight,
And I swear I saw a cat take flight.

Hot cocoa spills, but who needs a cup?
When marshmallows float, we just drink it up.
Our hearts are aglow, our spirits unwind,
In winter's embrace, the best peace we find.

So let the bells jingle, let the lights flash,
Let's make merry, create a big splash!
With laughter and love we'll celebrate cheer,
Hearts alight, it's our favorite time of year!

Together Under the Northern Lights

We bundled up tight, a sight to behold,
Warming our feet as the night turned cold.
With hot hands clutched, we dared to gaze,
At the twinkling lights that set our hearts ablaze.

The sky put on quite the cosmic show,
We laughed at the bears, 'Where do they go?'
Penguins doing salsa, just what we need,
In this brisk wonderland, we happily proceed.

Under the stars, we tell silly tales,
Of ice cream monsters and snail-sized whales.
With giggles and grins, we make our own cheer,
Together we shine, there's nothing to fear.

So here's to the nights, with icy delight,
Where joy dances freely, and dreams take flight.
We won't soon forget this frosty affair,
Together we sparkle, a magical pair!

Golden Moments in a Frosty World

The sun peeks out, a golden ball,
Making us feel ten feet tall.
Sledding down hills with snowballs in tow,
Every fall met with laughter and glow.

We chase winter birds, who tease and play,
Stealing our hats, what a cheeky display!
Frosty the snowman's got style so rare,
In shades and a vest, he's quite the affair.

Every breath a cloud, we giggle and shout,
Here's hoping this bliss never runs out!
Hot apple cider waiting back home,
With cookies that vanish like snowflakes that roam.

In this frosty world, we cherish each laugh,
Like mushing a puppy with care, not a gaff.
Golden moments cherished, frost-kissed delight,
Every memory sparkles, glowing so bright!

Taste of Gingerbread and You

In the kitchen, the chaos is sweet,
Flour on my face, oh, what a feat!
Gingerbread men with gumdrop eyes,
Runaway cookies, they're quite the surprise.

I mix and I stir, it's a sticky affair,
Can't help but laugh 'cause I've flour everywhere.
Adding more spice, oh, what could go wrong?
Maybe I'll bake a giant gingerbread song!

The oven's a trap for a sweet, warming scent,
But oh my, these goodies, they're nearly spent!
We chomp and we crunch with utter delight,
As crumbs start to fall, we take flight.

Sharing sweet treats, with a wink and a grin,
I'll take a bite, then let the fun begin!
Here's to gingerbread and moments so true,
Each bite's a reminder, I'm lucky with you.

Radiant Smiles on Frosted Windows

Frosted panes, a marvelous sight,
Smiles appear, oh what delight!
Snowmen dance in the chilly breeze,
While hot cocoa warms us with ease.

Laughter echoes through the air,
As we build snow forts with flair.
Sledding down hills, we tumble and slip,
Joyful screams make our hearts flip!

But mom wants no snowball fights here,
So we sneak and plan with good cheer.
Bumbles and giggles, a messy affair,
Radiant smiles everywhere!

Frosty friends, we laugh and play,
Creating memories day by day.
With rosy cheeks and spirits bright,
These winter days bring pure delight.

Enchanted Evenings by the Hearth

By the fire, the shadows dance,
Hot chocolate spills—oh what a chance!
Marshmallows float, sweet and white,
As we roast them late into the night.

Socks mismatched, a cozy look,
Muffled sounds from a good book.
Cats curling up, all snuggled tight,
While we giggle 'til morning light.

Trying to tell ghost stories grand,
But end up laughing, just as planned.
With s'mores in hand, we own the dark,
Enchanted evenings leave their mark!

With tales of yore and silly rhymes,
These moments will echo through all times.
As embers fade and our eyes grow dim,
We cherish these nights, which never seem grim.

Cherished Memories Wrapped in Joy

In the attic, boxes pile high,
Dusty treasures that make us sigh.
Old photo albums, laughter preserved,
Each page turned, a memory served.

Forgotten toys and games we played,
The silly pranks that never weighed.
Those awkward moments and goofy trends,
Cherished memories with dear old friends.

The time the cake fell on the floor,
Or when we danced, not caring whom we bore!
Each laughter ring brings joy in waves,
Wrapped tightly in love, our hearts it saves.

As years roll on, we sometimes sigh,
Yet in our hearts, these moments lie.
With jumbled laughter and happy tears,
We celebrate life and all its gears!

Tinsel Dreams and Laughter's Glow

Twinkling lights on a tree so bright,
Tinsel shines, a sparkling sight.
Ornaments clink, with stories to tell,
Of Christmas cheer, we know so well.

Caroling in the frosty air,
Voices raised, without a care.
Mismatched sweaters, cozy and snug,
Our holiday cheer, a warm, big hug.

Gingerbread houses, lopsided and fun,
With candies galore, we can't help but run!
Icicles hanging like drops of glee,
Tinsel dreams spark joy endlessly.

As laughter rings through every room,
We banish away the chill and gloom.
With hearts full of joy and spirits aglow,
Tinsel dreams and laughter's show!

A Cozy Evening Wrapped in Us

The blankets are piled, snug as a bug,
With popcorn in bowls, we'll both feel a hug.
The cats on the couch, snoring so loud,
We laugh at their dreams, oh, what a crowd!

The movie's a flop, we can't help but shout,
Our voices get loud, that's what it's about.
The cocoa is steaming, the marshmallows float,
We snuggle so close, like two silly goats!

The clock strikes too late, yet we still won't budge,
Just one more episode, oh, let's not judge!
With your hand in my hand, all worries are gone,
Let's cuddle forever, till the break of dawn!

So here's to our nights, both cozy and bright,
Wrapped in our warmth, everything feels right.
We'll laugh till it hurts, through thick and through thin,
A cozy evening, where love always wins!

Sweet Surprises Beneath the Tree

Under the tree, gifts piled so high,
I check every tag, what a sneaky spy!
The dog is all tangled in ribbons and bows,
While I search for cookies, you've hidden those!

A surprise from you, oh what could it be?
Maybe a training dart for the cat, we'll see!
Wrapped in bright paper, with sparkles galore,
I can't wait to find out what's hiding in store!

The cat takes a leap, knocks over a gift,
While laughter erupts, we both get a lift.
Each box brings a giggle, a joke or a snack,
I'm thinking of secrets, so you won't hold back!

Finally it's time, the moment's arrived,
We tear through the paper, joy can't be denied.
Sweet surprises await, with hugs in between,
This festive delight, what a hilarious scene!

Glow of Togetherness in Every Flake

The snowflakes are dancing, as crazy as us,
We shoveled the drive, but it caused a fuss.
With snowmen so goofy, they just want to fall,
We laugh as we build, they're not real at all!

In mittens and boots, we trudge through the white,
The hot chocolate brews, and things feel just right.
A snowball attack, the perfect retreat,
We giggle and tumble, cold noses we greet!

The glow of the lights on the tree shines so bright,
While we count snowflakes, creating our night.
I trip in the yard, face first in a pile,
But your laughter rings out and makes me just smile!

We've built our own world, no worries in sight,
In this winter wonderland, everything's light.
With snowflakes as witnesses, our spirit's awake,
Together we shine, with every fun flake!

Candlelight Shadows of Heartfelt Whispers

With candles aglow, the shadows do dance,
We sip on our drinks, share a spark and a glance.
The flickers of light create stories we weave,
In whispers we share, on this night we believe.

The music's a soundtrack, so soft in the air,
Each note wraps us close, as we both sit and stare.
You tell me a tale, I can't help but giggle,
As shadows become our own silly wiggle!

The dinner was fine, but dessert's a delight,
Chocolate and laughter, we savor each bite.
In candlelight's glow, our worries take flight,
With heartfelt whispers, everything feels right!

The clock keeps on ticking, but time's on our side,
We cherish these moments, with nowhere to hide.
With shadows and whispers, our hearts interlace,
In this cozy embrace, we've found our sweet place!

Snowflakes Dancing with Desire

Snowflakes flutter down, what a sight,
Like tiny dancers, oh, what a flight!
They twist and twirl in the frosty air,
Cotton candy kisses, without a care.

They whisper sweet nothings, cold as ice,
Hoping for warmth, oh, how nice!
Snowmen smile with a goofy grin,
As snowflakes smile, let the fun begin!

Making snowballs, oh what a throw!
Laughter erupts in the winter glow.
With cheeks so rosy, and noses red,
Those snowflakes dance in joy instead!

So grab your mittens, let's have a blast,
Snowflakes and laughter, let's make it last!
For in this chilly, wondrous dance,
Winter giggles, oh what a chance!

Evergreen Embraces Under Stars

Beneath the stars, the trees stand tall,
Evergreens whisper, come one, come all!
With branches wide, they stretch and sway,
Inviting all for a cozy play.

Squirrels giggle, having their fun,
While they toss acorns, one by one.
The moon winks down, giving a nod,
As fairies dance on soft, warm sod.

Twinkling lights give a sparkly hug,
Under the canopy, all snug as a bug.
Boughs laden with joy, can you believe?
These evergreen hugs, oh, let us weave!

So grab a friend and join the cheer,
In the forest's glow, there's nothing to fear.
With laughter and joy, the stars twinkle bright,
Evergreen embraces, all through the night.

Mistletoe Moments, Soft and Sweet

Oh, look up high, what do we see?
A sprig of mistletoe, just for thee!
With a cheeky grin and a playful glance,
It sets the stage for a clumsy chance.

Pucker up, it's that time of year,
Will you kiss me, or just disappear?
With hearts a-flutter, we fumble around,
In the heat of the moment, luck can be found!

Laughter erupts with each awkward peck,
We twirl and tease, oh, what the heck!
Wrapped in warmth, we share a sweet cheer,
Mistletoe moments, let's keep them near!

So dance underneath, let the giggles flow,
In this magical mistletoe glow.
With every soft kiss, our hearts take flight,
Mistletoe magic, oh, what a night!

Candlelit Dreams in Winter's Embrace

Candlelight flickers, casting a glow,
In winter's embrace, where whispers flow.
Dreams take flight on wings of the night,
As laughter echoes, oh what a sight!

Hot cocoa steaming, marshmallows afloat,
With each sip, we sail on joy's boat.
The warmth of the fire, its flickering flame,
Invites us to play a cozy, sweet game.

Snowflakes fall gently, a soft, sweet sound,
As friends gather 'round, love's warmth all around.
With stories and giggles, we weave our delight,
Candlelit dreams make everything bright!

So let the candles dance, twinkle and glow,
In winter's embrace, let your warmth flow.
With each heartfelt moment, let's sing with glee,
Candlelit dreams, a cheerful decree!

Ember-light Enchantment

In the hearth, the logs do dance,
A fire's glow, no second chance.
S'mores are stuck on fingertips,
Who needs a plate? We use our lips!

The cats plot schemes, with stealth and grace,
While we just hope to find our space.
Hot cocoa spills and marshmallows fly,
It's a wonder how we don't all cry!

The shadows twist in fiery glee,
As we debate the best way to pee.
Do we brave the cold or risk a drip?
Ah, the joys of a cozy trip!

With laughter loud and dodging sparks,
We serenade the squirrels and larks.
Ember-light will fade away,
But these memories here will always stay.

Frosted Flavors of Togetherness

In the kitchen, whisking like pros,
Mixing sprinkles, icing flows.
Sugar cookies shaped like cats,
We giggle hard, oh how we splat!

Frosting fights break out with glee,
One on the face? No, that's just me!
Flavors blend, a sweet ballet,
Together we bake the cares away.

Burnt edges? Well, who even cares!
We'll just cut up, share our shares.
These frosted delights, oh what a sight,
Happiness tastes oh-so right!

With plates stacked high, laughter spills,
Each bite is filled with joy and thrills.
In this kitchen, love's the spice,
Who knew desserts could feel so nice?

Joyous Tidings

Who spread the word that joy is near?
I tripped on tinsel - now that's cheer!
Snowflakes fall like confetti fun,
A winter party, everyone!

The carolers sing, off-key and proud,
A joyful melody, we cheer loud.
Each note a gift wrapped with giggles,
As we dance in our mismatched wiggles.

The tree is topped with a squirrel's tail,
Bright blinking lights, we laugh and rail.
Gifts piled high, with tape so sticky,
Unwrapping chaos, oh-so tricky!

As the night wraps us in delight,
We share our dreams, hold each other tight.
Joyous tidings, so silly and bright,
Who knew happiness could feel just right?

Silent Night's Promise

The snow falls softly, a cozy spell,
As I sit here with my cat, oh well.
We count the stars, and watch them twinkle,
While sipping tea, with a little wrinkle.

But wait, what's that? A sound, a crash!
Did Santa trip in the holiday bash?
I rush to peek, with a curious glance,
Oh dear me, it's just my pants!

Silent nights hold secrets deep,
Where dreams and giggles intertwine in sleep.
I make a wish on a falling star,
To keep the laughter, that's the best part!

So here's to nights where silence reigns,
And laughter dances in our veins.
With love and light, let's make a toast,
To silent nights, we love the most!

Milton Keynes UK
Ingram Content Group UK Ltd.
UKHW020344031224
452051UK00007B/170